To all our young readers as they race toward freedom

BLOOMSBURY CHILDREN'S BOOKS
Bloomsbury Publishing Inc., part of Bloomsbury Publishing Plc
1385 Broadway, New York, NY 10018

BLOOMSBURY, BLOOMSBURY CHILDREN'S BOOKS, and the Diana logo are trademarks of Bloomsbury Publishing Plc

First published in the United States of America in July 2024
by Bloomsbury Children's Books

Text copyright © 2024 by Amira Rose Davis and Michael G. Long
Illustrations copyright © 2024 by Charnelle Pinkney Barlow

Bloomsbury books may be purchased for business or promotional use. For information on bulk purchases please contact Macmillan Corporate and Premium Sales Department at specialmarkets@macmillan.com

Library of Congress Cataloging-in-Publication Data
Names: Davis, Amira Rose, author. | Long, Michael G., author. | Pinkney Barlow, Charnelle, illustrator.
Title: Go, Wilma, go! : Wilma Rudolph, from athlete to activist / written by Amira Rose Davis and Michael G. Long ; illustrated by Charnelle Pinkney Barlow.
Description: New York : Bloomsbury Children's Books, 2024.
Summary: The true story of how Olympic athlete Wilma Rudolph became a change-making civil rights activist.
Identifiers: LCCN 2023051418 (print) | LCCN 2023051419 (e-book)
ISBN 978-1-5476-1209-3 (hardcover) • ISBN 978-1-5476-1210-9 (e-pub) • ISBN 978-1-5476-1211-6 (pdf)
Subjects: LCSH: Rudolph, Wilma, 1940–1994—Juvenile literature. | African American women sprinters—United States—Juvenile literature.
Sprinters—United States—Juvenile literature. | African American women civil rights workers—Juvenile literature. | Civil rights workers—
United States—Juvenile literature. | LCGFT: Biographies. | Picture books.
Classification: LCC GV1061.15.R83 D38 2024 (print) | LCC GV1061.15.R83 (e-book) | DDC 796.42092 [B]—dc23/eng/20231107
LC record available at https://lccn.loc.gov/2023051418
ISBN 978-1-5476-1209-3 (hardcover) • ISBN 978-1-5476-1210-9 (e-book) • ISBN 978-1-5476-1211-6 (e-PDF)

The art for this book was created with handpainted cut-paper collage and various
mixed-media, with some finishes done in Procreate and Photoshop.
Typeset in Roboto Slab and Sunbeat Strong
Book design by John Candell
Printed in China by C&C Offset Printing Co., Ltd., Shenzhen, Guangdong
2 4 6 8 10 9 7 5 3 1

To find out more about our authors and books visit www.bloomsbury.com and sign up for our newsletters.

WILMA RUDOLPH, FROM ATHLETE TO ACTIVIST

GO, WILMA, GO!

written by
Amira Rose Davis
and **Michael G. Long**

illustrated by
**Charnelle
Pinkney Barlow**

BLOOMSBURY
CHILDREN'S BOOKS
NEW YORK LONDON OXFORD NEW DELHI SYDNEY

Wilma looks calm, but her heart is racing.
She crouches into position.
BANG!

The runners around her bolt away,
leaving her behind.

But Wilma's legs are long and strong.

Pumping her arms, she catches up.
Go, Wilma, go!

Stretching out her legs, she keeps pace.
Go, Wilma, go!

Digging in her cleats, she takes the lead.
Go, Wilma, go!

Pushing off her left leg, she soars across the finish line.

Wilma wins!

After the Olympics, where she won *three* gold medals,
Wilma tours Greece, England, and Germany.

At a beach near Athens, all kinds of people swim together.

Back in Wilma's hometown of Clarksville, Tennessee,
the community pool forbids Black people from swimming.

On a double-decker bus in London, all kinds of people ride together.

Back home in Clarksville,
bus drivers send Black people
to the back of the bus.

At a neighborhood café in Berlin,
all kinds of people eat together.
In Clarksville, restaurants won't
serve Black people.

Wilma tells a reporter: "In America, they push me around because I'm a Negro. Here in Europe, they push me to the front."

Wilma's comments shock many Americans, but she won't stop. *Go, Wilma, go!*

Back in Clarksville, the town leaders plan a celebration—a "Wilma Rudolph Day"—to welcome their champion home.

Wilma can't wait to see her friends and family, especially her daughter, Yolanda, who's already two years old!

But when she hears about Wilma Rudolph Day, Wilma **stops.**

She tells the town leaders that . . .

She won't go!

She won't go to Wilma Rudolph Day—
unless the leaders include Black people in
everything, in the parade and the banquet.
Wilma's demand shocks the leaders,
but she digs in.

Down the road in Nashville, restaurants have started serving Black people after months of lunch counter sit-ins.

Wilma thinks Clarksville should catch up.
What will the town's leaders do?
Will they have Wilma Rudolph Day without Wilma Rudolph?

"Go, Wilma, go!"
Thousands of fans line the street.
Black people and white people march side by side
in the Wilma Rudolph Day parade.

The all-Black Burt High band blares.
Wilma's parents ride in a fancy car.
Wilma waves from atop the back seat of a
sporty white convertible.

There's the lifeguard from the pool that's
off-limits to Black people.
And the bus driver who tells Black
people to move to the back.
And the restaurant owner who
refuses to serve Black people.

At the end of the parade, people pour into the community hall.

Black people and white people sit side by side at the Wilma Rudolph Day banquet.

After dessert, Wilma goes . . .

WILMA RUDOLPH DAY

. . . to the speaker's podium!
She looks calm, but her
heart is racing.

"In every effort," she says, "I have been motivated by one thing—to do justice to those who believe in me and to use my physical talents to the glory of God and the honor of womanhood."

The crowd is quiet, especially Clarksville's leaders. She had to push and pull them toward this moment.

"Winning the 100-meter . . . was the thrill of my lifetime," Wilma says. "My feelings then are matched only by my feelings now upon being welcomed home by so many friends."

The banquet hall erupts in cheers.

Go, Wilma, go!

In the years after Wilma Rudolph Day,
the community pool is still segregated.
So are the buses and the restaurants.

As her daughter Yolanda grows, so does Wilma's desire for change.

Wilma is steadfast and strong.
And she'll keep pushing and pulling and protesting . . .

. . . because the race to freedom is not a sprint—
It's a marathon!
Let's go!

AUTHORS' NOTE

Wilma Rudolph was born just outside of Clarksville, Tennessee, on June 23, 1940. Clarksville, like most of the South, was a racially segregated society. Laws and customs, known as "Jim Crow," enforced segregation. This meant that there were separate schools, hospitals, churches, playgrounds, and even water fountains for white people and Black people. Yet separate did not mean equal. Under Jim Crow, Black people were treated like second-class citizens.

As a child, Wilma was sick with polio, scarlet fever, and bouts of pneumonia. This made her small, weak, and unable to walk. In the Jim Crow South, especially in rural areas like Clarksville, it was hard for Black people to get good medical care. Fortunately for Wilma, Meharry Medical College was in Nashville, forty-five minutes away.

Meharry was the best medical school and hospital for Black people at the time. Black nurses and doctors came from all over to study and work at Meharry. Wilma and her mother traveled to the hospital on a segregated bus, where they were forced to sit in the back. Together they rode ninety miles, round trip, so Wilma could get the care she needed. The doctors thought she would never walk again, but when she was twelve years old, Wilma took off her leg braces and started to run.

Wilma played basketball and track, and she was so quick that everyone called her "Skeeter." Even when she was too young to attend college, her speed caught the attention of Ed Temple, the track coach of Tennessee State University. A historically Black college in Nashville, Tennessee State boasted the best women's track program in the country. At a time when many colleges did not have sports for women, Black schools in the South stood out because of the opportunities they provided women athletes. Tennessee State offered summer training camps, scholarships, and travel to out-of-state competitions.

As a high schooler, Rudolph began to run track with the Tennessee State program. Her early successes landed her a spot on the relay team heading to the 1956 Olympics in Melbourne. Wilma and three teammates would each run 100 meters, passing the baton around the track as quickly as possible. At fifteen years old and just a few years removed from wearing her leg braces, Rudolph competed in her first Olympic games and earned a bronze medal. Two years later, she gave birth to her first daughter, Yolanda. With support from her family, she continued to go to school and pursue her dreams. Wilma trained for the next Olympic games and her hard work paid off! In 1960 she was chosen to represent the United States at the Olympics in Rome, Italy.

Traveling the world greatly impacted Wilma. For the first time in her life, she found herself outside the Jim Crow South. As she competed in other countries, she started to question why she was treated so differently outside the United States. After winning three gold medals at the 1960 Summer Olympics in Rome, signing autographs for fans, and listening to people cheer her name, Wilma said: "In America, they push me around because I am a Negro. Here in Europe, they push me to the front" ("Olympic Girl Champ Dreads Coming Home," *New York Amsterdam News*, September 10, 1960). In Europe, Wilma's car was guarded by dogs because so many fans were excited to see her. But back home in Tennessee, police were turning dogs on Black college students like her who were marching for civil rights.

Across the country, young people were protesting Jim Crow laws. They were marching, boycotting, and voting. In Nashville, Diane Nash and other students organized sit-ins to desegregate lunch counters. Wilma's experience abroad and the energy of the growing civil rights movement at home fueled her decision to speak out against a segregated parade and banquet in Clarksville. Although Wilma Rudolph Day in 1960 became the first integrated event in Clarksville, Jim Crow continued to flourish there. Clarksville's public facilities, including parks and the local swimming pool, remained segregated. Many private businesses also continued to enforce Jim Crow laws and customs.

Yet Wilma persisted as well. She was increasingly determined to use her platform to protest racial inequality. Wilma was part of a generation of Black athletes in the United States who were raising their voices to question the status quo. Because of the country's love of sports, and all the glory that came with winning, Black athletes like Wilma and her friend Muhammad Ali understood that they had a powerful platform from which to speak.

The more she traveled for track, the more Wilma learned about Black people around the world fighting for equality—even in those cities in Europe that had seemed so welcoming to her at first. She visited places like Dakar and Ghana and began to think about a global Black community, connected in struggle and solidarity. Her travels made her even more determined to return to Tennessee and fight for change.

For Wilma, it was important to speak out, but it was also important to *act*. Three years after Wilma Rudolph Day, and a few weeks after returning from West Africa, she protested racial segregation at a Clarksville restaurant named Shoney's. Wilma and other activists peacefully assembled in front of the restaurant multiple times over two days. Local white residents heckled and harassed them. About a week later, Clarksville's city council voted to integrate Shoney's and all public facilities in the city. It was another gold-medal victory for Wilma.

Wilma continued to decry racism and sexism long after her victories in Clarksville.

She advocated for Black girls and women to have opportunities in sports and beyond in everything she did. And Wilma did a lot. She started a foundation, coached track, served on presidential councils, and wrote a memoir.

In summer 1994, Wilma was diagnosed with aggressive brain cancer. She passed away four months later at just fifty-four years old.

Today, if you visit Clarksville, you will drive into town on the same roads that the old, segregated bus rolled down. Be sure to look at the street signs. You just might see Wilma Rudolph Boulevard. And if you stop by the Wilma Rudolph Event Center, you will view the bronze statue of the Olympian, arms swinging, mid stride, racing toward her goals, while firmly planted in a hometown that she helped transform.

You can also see her rich legacy in a new generation of Black athletes who are raising their voices about injustice. Black women athletes, like Wilma Rudolph before them, are leading the way. From Olympian Gwen Berry to tennis player Naomi Osaka to the numerous WNBA players, Black women athletes are using their platforms to speak out about racism, sexism, homophobia, and the stigma of mental illness. Occasionally, their contributions are overlooked, but, like Wilma, they remain resolute in their desire to advocate for change. Wilma would be proud.